Lie Down with Me

Lie Down with Me

NEW AND SELECTED POEMS

Julie Suk

Autumn House Press

PITTSBURGH

Autumn House Press Staff
Editor-in-Chief and Founder: Michael Simms
Managing Editor: Adrienne Block
Community Outreach Director: Michael Wurster
Co-Founder: Eva-Maria Simms
Fiction Editors: Sharon Dilworth, John Fried
Associate Editor: Rebecca King
Assistant Editor: D. Gilson
Media Consultant: Jan Beatty
Publishing Consultant: Peter Oresick
Tech Crew Chief: Michael Milberger
Intern: Caroline Tanski

Autumn House Press receives state arts funding support through a grant from the Pennsylvania Council on the Arts, a state agency, through the Pennsylvania Partners in the Arts (PPA), its regional arts funding partnership. State government funding depends upon an annual appropriation by Pennsylvania's General Assembly and from the National Endowment for the Arts, a federal agency. PPA is administered in the Pittsburgh region by the Greater Pittsburgh Arts Council.

ISBN: 978-1-932870-55-8
Library of Congress Control Number: 2011912293

..... Contents

From *The Medicine Woman* (1980)

From *Heartwood* (1991)

From *The Angel Of Obsession* (1992)

From *The Dark Takes Aim* (2003)

. . . . . New Poems

which explains why we shiver
when the heedless stars swing by.

Come see,
says my son,
the lens of his telescope
momentarily focused

beyond
what I want to believe—

that the earth is not
the last place we touch,
our song whisper rant
not drifting off
without route or shore.

I trace lines but find
no discernible shape for Vesta
Omega Aquarius Cetus

no trail marked
THIS IS THE WAY,

nothing
of anger sorrow love
or the foolish wishes
we wept and fought for

not knowing they seldom
come true, hope
the most savage lie.

And there in the lower sky,
Venus—

no, a night flight
flashing through trees
and beyond,
and I'm not aboard,

am left, you could say,
like the aura of a burned-out star,

the body,
that incorrigible flirt,
still leading me on.

I love the *louche* look
of Caravaggio's Eros
staring at me with a wicked grin.

He rises, half out, half in
the bed, one knee bent on the edge,

so irresistible it's easy
to forget the blood-caked arrowheads
scattered across the floor.

En garde, I warn the mirror,
and fall into my rumpled life,
gown hiked, feelings sprawled wide,
the room splattered with moonlight.

Chiaroscuro hollows the body,
each *misterioso* splotch
a cave I can't wait to explore,

scavenging for the treasure,
scooping it up close
Mine! Mine!

and so devoured.

Therefore, Mortal, Prepare for Yourself an Exile's Baggage

Ezekiel 12:3

Hard words, old man.
I want to hear what I don't necessarily believe.

Tell me the life I'm leafing through now
has a spectacular end—pushed out ablaze,
weeping and wailing on shore, my final words sizzling.

Never mind that the living turn toward tomorrow.
Hurry! The day's on the table, and getting cold.

Tell me scraps of memory last
longer than the people who pass them on.

Tonight the moon hangs so close I swear
it could drop into my arms.

This heart still fibrillates despite the rational ribs.

I don't want to hear what I know is true,
that Voyager, with a capsule of me and you, wanders
in a fathomless sea, no handouts, no drawing ashore.

The stars with no one on board have nothing to lose.

I do.

My luggage was packed soon as the world took me in
touching everything mine I believed I owned.

His plane was scarcely more than canvas
stretched across board.

Gunned down by a German Fokker onto no-man's land,
my father crawled under cross-fire to a crater
and sprawled in on the dead.

Only once did he mention the maggots and stench
in a world that slammed up too soon.

That night, between the sizzle of flares,
a Yank pulled him back into a trench and left
before the swapping of names.

Long after I came and went my ways, a friend of his
passed through town, bringing with him an army pal.
Buddy, old buddy, war tales told until what do you know—
true I swear true—they found it was the stranger
who'd rescued my father.

Crying, they embraced—life is so sweet
when death is on leave.

By spring a tumor invaded my father's brain,
taking him out, along with his wish to float
once just once again with the noiseless clouds.

I'm left replaying those summer nights
we sat on the stoop, bull-bats diving overhead,
cicadas puncturing the quiet.

See, he pointed, *there—there!* scorpion,
fish, ram and lyre, wheeling across a sky
threatened by hunter and bear.

Hiding my face on his arm, it was hard to connect
myth with the lap I nestled in.

And still no clue
from a heaven seemingly preoccupied.

Tracers that stutter around us
briefly illuminate our lives,

what I forgot to say, what I forgot to give
to the living, bringing me down to a fragment
of you, my derring-do father who flew.

Splayed against the window,
its moth powder sifts
through the screen.

The eyespot on each wing
blind as I was toward those I loved—

meaning the ghosts who still
mill around in my dreams.

The dust of rue
must have been terrible
for my 103-year-old grandfather,
wives and friends he outlived
haranguing his sleep.

A lovesick boy once threw pebbles
at my bedroom window.

Huddled in a cocoon of sheets
I refused his pleas,

afraid he might break
through my green will, afraid
of loss even before I took flight.

My mother at the mirror,
one finger circling her cheeks with rouge.

Don't cry, she says, *It puffs your eyes.*
Kiss your own bruise.

You soaked with rain,
a broken steering wheel in your hands.

A cold wind shook me awake,
our son recalled,
miles away when his father died.

Memento mori—
the nightmare not yet cool—
the child whose mind,
in the beginning, was lucid and whole.

Bit by bit we're exposed, earth,
piled over long-buried bones,
collapsing,

and there we are—
shrouds of the life we clung to
a vaporous scroll.

Remind me as often as it takes
to bury rue.

Let morning glisten
like the clear surface of childhood—

a canoe slipping through a black lagoon,
flushed ibis clattering from a sand bar.

The rift widens
and the skeletal past
tumbles into view.

This
the pelvis of a woman
the lip of a bowl.

This
a man an ax
shattered bones.

Once we were wholly ourselves
before wounds told on us.

This
my desk covered with shards
I can't restore.

The afternoon before you died
we watched the flickering TV screen
in your hospital room,

you staring somewhere beyond—

at the life we built on
or the life in ruins?

Should I have stayed that night?
Who knows the hour that has no chime.

Called before dawn—
I knew the ring.

If I had slept by your side
I would have held you
against the cold

wind blowing
we don't know where

over the house
over the ashes
over a round of stones.

Blades of sun slash the dark room,
a breeze slips out of nowhere
caressing my neck—you're after me again.

Any moment I could find myself mute,
passing through the living
with outstretched arms.

Your co-conspirator Brahms
and his alto rhapsody
luring me to turn myself in.

It's the play of your hands I miss.
Memory and its few sips of communion
fail to convert.

I clutch the sheets,
not yet ready for you to pull me over.

Maybe it's true
nothing in nature disappears
energy dispersing from one form to another.

When the dead float around us, hackles rise.
You never know who might be walking nearby.

Good grief Einstein, what happened to you!

Think eons of layovers and hosts,
a smattering of this or that,
nothing tribal.

Worse—the loss of flesh and touch,
like the acts of love we fall into and out.

Put your hand here
and here

the garden glistening with the greenest of greens,
you and I speaking in tongues.

What did I know—
barely sixteen, a not-yet-bruised
gardenia fixed to my hair.

Full of yourself, my cousin teased
as we rocked on clicking rails
into the city, into a ballroom

filled with smoke, the only light
a spangled sphere spun in flashing echos

. . . that stardust melody . . .

I whirled through
until he called
Enough!

As if there were ever enough.

Dragged home, wilted, crushed,
yet the stuff of stars,
or so it's said,

and look,

tonight the stars are falling, the dead
evaporating into particles and waves,

going out,
going cold,

my breath in your neck,
yours in my hair,

the stars wheeling on, on,
with or without our debris.

..... *Recall Me to the Memory*

Dante Alighieri

I'm dying and they will not speak of it, my grandmother wrote

on a yellowed slip of paper pressed
with flowers, a lock of hair, and ginkgo leaves,
between the pages of Canto XXV.

She played the piano, my father the violin.
Only thirteen he raged room to room the day she died.

The faded ginkgo leaf I hold against the window of the attic
fans into gold.

. . . a glow that met and passed . . .
is Dante's take.

Mine is in a letter I keep from a man I loved.

    Those tears—I'll never forget . . .

Back and forth, he and I confessing our lives.

Books, letters, strings, leaves —
perhaps it's true that the beat of the heart is the same
as the frequency of the universe.

Less than a drop of blood remains in me that does not tremble . . .
earth my body is, in earth . . .

    are words she underlined.

At night they graze lawn to lawn,
cloven hooves denting the soft loam.

New leaves, flower buds, seedlings—gone.

The body of a buck found crumpled
at a corner near the highway,
a twitch still playing the left hind leg.

Doe, fawn, stag—the many who drift by
and on, deserting us for the baleful
underground mission of worms.

Even the bees, gone, taking with them aromas
that drive the senses into rut—

the earthy, the salty, the gamey
odor I love of a man.

Wisp
of a feather caught on a twig.

On the ground, three
indigestible balls the owl regurgitates—

a compression of bones,
feathers, and bits of a beak dropped
from the oak where he roosts.

Goodbye to the nut-like contents
of a cardinal's brain.

Goodbye to the far-off wail of a train
rattling me awake, the past in flight,

leaving a twinge in my thighs,
though I lie with someone else.

You, a sort of hummingbird flash
through a dream
that continues haunting the day—

a disconnect between the scrawl
of words I wait to read,
and a hand poised mid-air.

About my father's decision
to raise chickens during the war:
my chore was to tend to the newly-hatched,

each morning a few found trampled and ground
into wires of the brooder cage, leaving me to toss
the flat yellow disks of down.

Take the hard with the soft of it, he advised, and I do—

the plush of a day,
the table set with candles and wine,
the sheets turned back, in case...in case...

a return of hands strumming my thighs,
a segue of strokes limb to limb,
the inquisitive tongue having its way.

In the fenced-in yard where chickens scratched,
I pampered a rooster named Keats.
Here, here, I called and he waggled
from his awkward strut to the cricket I waved.

One day a hawk, and that was the end.

Since then I've convinced myself—
for every crack in illusions, no tears,
no brooding, no flying the coop.

Here, Jules, take this, my father said,
lowering a damp new chick to my lap.

Under the wide willow tree, the child leads me by the hand.

This is my room, she says, *yours is over there,*
the bent limb your chair, and no ghosts allowed.

That means no abandoned dream knocking,
no walls between moans of love and daily routines,
no weeping in bed.

I pretend, as I always have, that the lives I've known
were real as the ones

drifting past, calling out my name before they fade—
a vapor, a gust, or a wake of fragrance melding into the next
I rush up to on the street,

mistaking his laugh for another's
once close as a prowling tongue in my ear.

Sweet, you murmured, *sweet*, your hands everywhere,
drawing me onto your knees

where I sat rapt and still—so still—afraid we might break.

Say this is what you've done—
rounds of errands, and visits,
a swing back home
to mop, dust, wash, eat,
the days before much the same,
vaporous as a dream.

Say the time it takes
in a dark garage to dash
from the car's interior
diminishing light to the door
of the house, the wrong key
fumbling the lock,

the rustle of fear that you aren't,
and never again will be, safe,
that time will steal your place,
your love, your grief.

If the day starts sweet
cloyingly sweet
like the first scent of a dead mouse
wasting behind a wall,

take a deep breath and hold,
death takes its own sweet time.

You
baiting a trap
in case sorrow and disaster
come paired,

and if the day is not
one you want remembered—

that drag, your shadow,
continuing to haunt
like an amputated limb—

isn't it better than tomorrow
suddenly bereft of you?

You could say
we're the dregs of stars

more visible on days
we suffer remorse

for the numberless
lacerating grit

of major harms
    and minor barbs
piled dune-high

    an edgy
        shifting

paths obliterated

you could say
intent running out

an O so hot
star exploding

likewise
our own small puff.

He needs your goodbye,
she said,
he was so fond of you.

I leaned over the bed
and barely pressed
a cheek to his—

cold
as a Dresden doll,

the mysterious
that rides us in sync,
no longer there.

What I fear:
sending the ones I love
off with an angry word,
maybe the last they hear.

Kiss him, she said.

And here's what I did as a child:
kept one folded hand
tucked in my arm pit—

warm

as all the hollows
I later shared
when the living found where I hid.

Don't think pitch-black. Concentrate
on the spectacular pictures shunted from space:

    stars sparking out of nebulae,
    galaxies spinning in billows of dust,
    earth a tremulous cell.

Don't think of the daily risk of incineration
by a flash of ill-will, the world rattling off its shelves,
nor of sorrow finding us where we hide
under the accessories of our lives,

    you and I tangled
    in the cold ending we don't want read,
    night dragging us into its senseless hole.

Concentrate on close-ups:

    The bead of water on my lip
    before your mouth finds mine.

Forget the wasp humped over the apple I bit,
the taste of pain hanging on.

Think of tomorrow on the rise.
Tomorrow we'll say what we meant.

It's hard to say what I mean,
talking to you, it seems,
from another room.

Yes, yes, while shaking my head.

Torn letters tack across an empty street,
the flap of an awning audible to no one.

Forgive the times I deserted our lives
so sure I was of finding myself.

You could say I drove off too fast,
scenery a quick-change artist,
the horizon fickle too.

You could say
truth was whispered so seldom and low
it echoed lies.

In my wake, a sprawl of lines
raced between hello and goodbye.

Forgive me for saying I'd heard it all.

Repent! a man on the corner shouts.
Apparently I'm doomed
to repeat the lessons I ran through,

and I'm not sure who's left to care,
but I loved you—I did—
each of you.

How we love those worlds
turned upside down
at holiday time.

The swirl of snow
in the thick glass globe falling
on village, skating rink, sleigh.

No smoke rising from chimneys,
no aromas, no flash of a bird,
no buzz of a fly,

each new settling of white the only change,
the figures miming a soundless world.

Here, we say, *here—words!*
and thrust them in as if words
could shake them to life,

and they do—the man on the sled
has another by the throat,
a frenzy of fists,
snow shuffled with red.

Foolish, the thought
of taking back what was said.

Snow on the drift again.

Each day the one hand washes its brother,
fingers finding a momentary link,
though we live one place, and dream another—

maybe to escape what we might uncover.
I didn't mean to! the man shouts at the sink,
one hand washing blood from its brother.

Aim, shoot to kill, is the given order.
The second round is easier than you think
if you live one place, and dream another.

Say, in our lives we prefer to wander
without thought of the ruin left in our wake—
night comes, and each hand must wash it brother.

Once by default I lost a son and daughter,
lost heart during their prodigal way back.
I lived one place, they dreamed another.

Each day I reason with nightmare and order,
ranging here, there, in a world out of sync.
Each day one hand washes its brother
while I dream one place, and live another.

You back me against the kitchen door
and whisper in my ear,

Put the knife down.
Let the world simmer on its own.

We wash and wring our telltale hands:

no tracking the day
through the house,
no gore scraped on the doorsill,

no explosives
strapped around the wind
lifting the leaves
that cover our most private fears,

but soon enough the door slams
against the wall and disquiet spills
into the room.

On the outskirts a child wails,
darkness running amok,
the horizon on fire.

The past clatters off and leaves us stranded
in the desert of a new century,
our pale and inconclusive trial of dust
collapsing.

You point to this hour or that
reminding me how I wept and raged.

Now darkness diminishes those days,
the stars bearing down
on the accident of our being

as if they cared.

Our only warmth—
the fires we build in the body.

Will we wake to a cooler sun? Will we wake?

Death, an anesthesia, no color,
no core, no scent.

Rock me once more on your knees.
Tell me the story you say we lived.

Not that I believe the lies,
but your breath is so sweet,
your hands rippling over me.

The moon stalls in the limbs of the sweet gum,
and I'm hung up in a nightmare I can't shake loose—
a black dog dead at the end of a tether.

I swaddle the body in a sweater and rock it in my arms.
Wake, dog, wake, I croon but a grimace hardens his face.

Night bulges with ghosts racing to no end.
That's why I sleep holding on to you
even as our covers slip to the floor
and the room cools.

My worst fear: the heat of the body is a brief dew
the senses can't follow.

Tomorrow time moves up and I lose another hour.

But here comes daylight—rose under black,
a gap between silence and applause,
the intricate strings of the body still playing.

A binocular sweep finds him hunched
poker-faced in the crotch of the oak,

each fur-like feather outlined, same as the eyes,
the head swiveling slow-motion

to a movement on the lawn below.
Dive! I say, *Dive!*

before it's too late. I know how it is
to move in close and lose the take.

It's dusk, and I miss
all but the fluttering leaves

that describe his passage down.
A guttural shriek connects with flesh,

tufts of rabbit pelt ripped,
the belly slit by talon and beak,

glistening entrails and the still stricken eyes
wrenched out gurgling.

Here death is defined, not shrouded in lies.
Here guts and stench insist

I not turn away. Night swoops at my back.
May clover fill my mouth to the end.

..... from *The Medicine Woman*

The tribe of fleas we dropped,
now a civilization
that went on without us.

But not too far.
Perhaps the next tomb
or the mound we're buried in
tempered with beads, feathers, and flesh.

Or closer—
the rattle of a spear when you shift against me,
the hand holding an axe,
the arm which might be mine,
the carbon's tick
ticking us off.

So close something is bound to turn up.
Perhaps the faint glow of residue
sinking with our bones.
Perhaps something I can tap loose
from this jar.
something I feel now
stirring inside,

close as dust on a wing
close as the feeler
slipping through a crack.

I

My father
My mother
The rock
The tree

I wove a nest in the crook of an arm
Where I brood

Warm enough to open
Soft enough to feather and sing

II

When the vision appears
No arrow can stop the flight
That lands with me
Feathered in its claws
And the forest I enter
Is a shadow of the one I leave
Trees look solid but are not
Nothing is held or hard
Lights spill into other lights
A river of sun shakes its scales
Edges crumble into currents
Every crevice eaten out
I look at the world through a waterfall
And the world floats

III

When I see darkness I see you
Running beneath a cloud
And the field left dry
I see your blood slough shadow
There is nothing to bury when you die

You love death
You lie in its cave
Strung tooth and claw to pelt
The body an open grave

But the dead prowl
Your woman wanders a desert
And the desert blankets your child
And under the blanket is a stone
And the stone melts
The child drowning in its fire

You come to me for a cure
Slipping in under the night
You lift my skin with your blade

Again you bear down
And I bleed

Crazy woman you say
Lick my sores
And I open my mouth

They were feeding my father soup when he died.
None of us was there to hold the spoon.
All those months under a hospital cap
he refused to take off, determined to play
"gin rummy" though he rarely knew who I was
waiting for his brain to discard.

He was born with six fingers on each hand,
the extras chopped off, flaps stitched.
What's that? I asked, discovering scars.
Someone inside tried to claw out
but lost hold and fell, was the story he told.

I had nightmares of that other one
scrabbling frantically before dropping from sight.

After my mother died, I swung
back and forth between his world and mine.
Cluttered years, glimpses over candles and silver.
Yes, I'm happy. Yes, the children are fine.
It was hard to catch my father for long.

Sometimes I go to bed scared
of not coming through, the night
full of the radiant falling into themselves,
fragments curving back,
a drop of sweat, a single pulse,
felt as they were moments ago.

No wonder I sleep close
Your mouth to my breast
A moon still throbbing
Your pulse in my flesh

Our nights spent
Hanging on edge
While darkness pushes us out

No wonder we drift

The slow motion of feathers
Settling in a windless house

All our lives spun on collapse
Sucked through a rip so black
We fling ourselves to the ground
And hold on

One hand tethered
The other slapping at the dark

As we listen
For light crackling
And a voice sent back.

I dream of stones
and stumbling through them
a lost child lovers a stray
finding a field
and at the far end
a wild fading clump of a barn
    the kind you cut a finger to own
    and sign in blood.

There is more shuttered in and out of sequence:
    the fragrance of damp bodies bumping into sleep
    from the loft a shout
    murmurs feathering down
    and myself
    lying here weathered.

Minutes hours years later
the barn burns and I wake
on fire to rush in and save what I can:
    the lost children who still hide
    abandoned and closed
    the children who have grown to be mine
    and the lover I slept through
    while my ashes lifted with the wind
    and died.

This is what it means to rain
and hard ground not hold.
This is how it is to be a fern
pressed into stone.

A man I could love wanders by and touches me.
I throw myself in his eyes.
He leans on me
but the ashes are spread too thin
and he passes through.

I settle where I can.

A pine-still night presses needles through sleep.
Not enough wind to carry the clouds.

Moon
Catching the leaves
That whisper in hollows.

Lost
Wax to your metal
And you where I want

The two of us sweetgrass
Woven to hold
The buried
Familiar.

Heart pumping
As if it had pipes through the wilderness.

Touch teaches catch as catch can
but heave, grind, kiss or whine
put you nowhere near the body's pith;
when mimosa furls,
the frond holds a private air,
and rumors, true or not,
flock the mind we puzzle,
and fade in a territory
fenced by words.

It is the mole,
swimming in his shallow hole,
who knows dark as a depth
he parts with as he goes,
one arm forward, palm facing out,
a push back,
the other arm brought
in front of his snout.

Shaping towards day,
we wonder at whose house
the dog barks through the night.
Answer, answer ruins our sleep
until the light turns him out.

The hunt
down to bulbs in summer,
in autumn acorns.

Not a tissue of smoke, no spear
or remnant of rope.
His footprints, leaves
backed into stone.

Found: ash scattered through stubble.

Ishi Ishi
voice never sighted.

Learned to sign his name and collect.
Learned that where we walked
the twig cracked.

Song written on sand:

  Where will I go?
  Whom will I ask?
  An arrow enters the dream.
  Under the mask, another
  holds my breath
  cornered
  A surface of names
  blurs one on another.
  The eyes of doe and fawn close.

I will grow old in this house.
A forest for crows.

He died
and was buried in the manner.

From the beginning,
driven over a precipice
and eaten raw.

Devoid of council,
what could we hold but autopsy?

Old man.
Old man,
even the films we took went bad.

At the end of the block
a transformer halts for a moment
before continuing its hum.

It seems a moth crossed the lamp—
the way we read the world
   a dark room
   flickering light,
   dust floating
   transfused.

I lie here conjuring faces of people I love.
No wonder I sleep clinging to your back.
How can we sleep at all
thinking of the dreams lined up
to be filled—
   parents, lovers
   and the children we pass
   as if they were strangers,
   our minds on something else.

Even now your face dissolves.
Sleepless I prowl room to room
   a feverish cat
aching for secrets I nursed
and drowned.

The woods grapple with fog,
thoughts immediate as crows on snow
feed in a cluster.

In a library, sleek burgundy chairs
I once slid on
like a seal through water.

From Bavarian lamp globes
blood-light flowed.
Red was a cave of color
in the book, *Paradise Lost.*

What hell hurled down
to flame his brain?

No other clutched
my thoughts as much
as he who plummeted
from my years.

Beneath the surface red flowed
through conversation. *Careful,*
careful, don't tell her.

Some things seem to splatter
more when spilled. Milk is one.
Blood, another.

I'm surprised we've come this far.
Frayed ends ravel every step of the day.
You can't walk down the street without a glimpse
of the case of mistaken identity
you rush to meet—
was the face always this cold,
the hero this tyrant?

A woman with scarred wrists contemplates her throat.
"This time," she tells herself, "I'll spill
and be memorable."

Like a rabbit running to death,
entrails spinning from a hole in his gut,
what feeling can we possibly hold
when a nine-year-old villager in cut-down fatigues
throws a grenade?
    Rule one: if you shoot don't weep.
    A shot is like a particle of light
    which is also a wave,
        which proves we haven't put it together.

Beyond our wreck of curiosity,
stars thin and pile again. Again
the eye registers a dead light.
No wonder we collide.

Even now your son and mine race down a dark street
toward a barricade neither is prepared to break.
Our remnants shuttle across lives.
The loom spins out, picking up threads.
Who will we wear?

The exact name slips
Miss Elise Miss Fanny Miss Aleta Jane
whoever they call mad
a compulsive walker
every morning at eight
the same crepe dress
frazzled as moss
ribbon at the throat
beaded bag
and circling her head
the wide-wheeled galaxy
of an infinitely purple hat
every morning at eight
down the crumbling steps
past columned houses
infested by glories
snarled back on their seed
every morning dogs
railed against chains
dogs at her heels
dogs at the drugstore hardware trolley
dogs sprawled at the feet of old cronies
don't pay her no mind
she don't bother nobody
every morning to the dock
past honky-tonks latticed porches
whores rocking their grievances
back uptown to the square
three times around through pigeon flocks
scattered lord knows where

the route lost until five
when she showed for a tray
from whoever they call kind
every day the same
rarely spoke
never complained
walked as they said
to her grave
and we still look for the ghost
the dogged
crazed to tear loose
Miss Elise Miss Fanny Miss Aleta Jane

Madness is a precarious ridge.
Hackles rise when we least expect.
A scream slips from the edge of a cliff
and falls, forest and fog in ascent,
the tree-line pitched,
wolves howling down the spine:

the way smoke spirals from a log
until coals slump into cracks and catch.

Wolf eyes: Topaz,
garnet at night,
deep burns turned hard.

When the moon thins,
and breasts tighten,
the wolf gnaws out of his cage
to roam my flesh.

His cry leaps from a pit as we roll
and romp on a lawn of pelt.

When the howl swells to a held-high pitch,
I can hear his whimpering mate
tear at the wire with her bleeding mouth.

What do you say to the cat
when you slam the door on his tail?

He's starved to translate
even a scrap,
howling as if in heat
and the neighborhood spayed.

All I can do is rub.
We live on touch.

Once after a storm
I found newly hatched whelks
washed up on the beach—
hundreds clinging to rotten kelp.

The sea pulls out
and leaves fossils in the yard.
What we know of them is hard.

I'm only human
you explain
switching the room from light to dark.

Outside
a peeping-tom fogs the glass
and signs his name.

Noguchi went wild
when he saw the steel mill
of Sloss Sheffield.

To him
it was the best piece in town,
no klutzy columned pile of bricks,
but stacked!

and he wanted to paint them
in primaries
when nothing comes true,
not blonde or brunette.

That crazy great Isamu—
imagine,

blue, yellow, and bawdy red
phallic conceits
rising from the concrete.

Mind you,
these are serious considerations
city fathers beget
in our centers.

They pulled Jackie from the wax museum
but not Marilyn.
Like the Alabama congressman said,
Everything is made for love.

It was an archaeologist named Love
who found a piece of Aphrodite
in a basement storage room.

Like you I want to be uncovered.

It's *Find me, find me,*
complete this form.

You dig
and more bodies pour into the tombs
but something is missing,
the ancient desert sucked dry,
its marrow replaced by stones.

You recover what you can.
The catalogue lists
amulets, reliefs, charms,
a mummy-form staring under lapis lazuli,
and inside the case
the dry, shriveled remnant
once called King.

Down here it's back and forth,
the spirit restless and still no home.

Do you realize how close you've come?
I wear my face hoping you'll find me.
Everything I've buried wants out

to taste your breath,
and in your hands
wake spiced and oiled.

No use to question stars,
the answer could be off
by the time it reaches us.

One crack and out,
you wedged between darkness and sun-up,
my side of the bed still warm.

Outside on the lawn
random prints evaporate.

Tracking through the body,
the same wilderness as before—
savage, few clearings,
fires out of control.

Again you ram down the stake.
I'm kept by the house.
A note under the door reads,
Came by but you were asleep.

A fifth of our life is spent on dreams.
Veins hum with the motion of stars.
one ear tuned in,
the mouth ringing
hello, hello...

Floating in
  rushing out
we tangle
but nothing holds fast.
A message might drift for years
and never come back

yet I still
throw myself out
  imagining you on the shore
  imagining me in your hands.

Is it possible to land
  finally
on one thing we love?

I know I'm only half-filled
  a pocket a groove
  collector of drift
holding what I can

of earth
that even now gives

the voice I could drown in
murmuring off
in the dark.

I halve an apple on the radius
and discover a star-shaped center.
At the flowering end of the apple
you see the same star
only pulled in

the way a turtle snaps back
frightened
into puckered skin,

the way we clutch what we own
Don't touch! Don't touch!
as if this was likely
swathed as we are.

This inner start is open,
full of seeds
jumbled like miniature boats
left in an ancient tomb
long since forgotten.

Everywhere hunger,
ferryboat seeds going out
coming back
oarless,

the life inside
waiting to be rescued.

If the dream has nothing to do with life
but crouch on the night-side
and blink at our traffic
why are we time and again
blinded and hit?

When I rise from sleep,
I look back at the map of lines
strewn across darkness.

Roads eventually dip into a hub—
these ruins, that trace
of an old trail once deep in ruts
now disappearing.

Now and then death erupts
tossing up every grotesque twist.

Deeper
I can feel stones shift
as if over the burial of someone still alive,
no doubt unbearable thirsty
and running out of breath.

I give what I have,
and give
mouth to mouth.

On the edge of the Antarctic shelf
ice fish breathe through skin.

Eyes crystal, nearly invisible,
they have no protective scales.
When they move through water,
water swims.

In a world of floats
I hang where I can.

Ice forms around sleep
holding my wake.

Fish, eat me out.
Don't tell me the terrible,

that we die preserved in ice,
no melt,
and dream what we feel.

Pressed against ice,
lips frozen
on the multiple mirrors
curved in, no out,

I want you the length of me,
the salt of you rubbed on my skin.
I ache watching you swim.

*Launched from Cape Canaveral, the spacecraft
carries with it messages from Earth.*

If you look up at night
you might think of it drifting there
without moorings among the stars,
the hold filled with treasures,
a whale's song on the reel.

Grounded by time,
we shave off yesterday's shadow
and move into traffic.

The hope is we'll be found,
if not whole at least an imprint,
perhaps an ancient boat, oarlocks intact
a golden prow.

The vision we keep is heroic:
a ship and pyre headed out
trailing rope, the body still burning
when it arrives.

The whale's echo could overflow
a billion years, sounding
until it drowns.

Or it could split the sky
and out of the spray
find tongue.

Any day you could be swept off by the river.
Any day shift and crumble.

If a foot presses you inward,
if you're lifted out and thrown to the wheel,
at least pain shapes to the rest of life.

You have it in you to be held.
You know the hand, how it smooths and roots.
Wet with longing, what will you save?

You know the mouth and all it can open.
You know the feel of its petals
and how we're transported by the hum.

The river comes a long way to pool.
You have it in you to flower.

They came up-river
lugging baskets of dirt to patches of land
lost in swamp and palmetto,
the mound building up to gods,
the drum calling to the mask
the body dancing out of shadow.

What signals they lit are out,
the low grave mounds pocked by shovels,
midden plundered, the spirit scattered,
and now we come to piece the cup.

No telling how deep the body is flexed
in its grave. Where the body is
there is also treasure. And bones,
the beautiful bones that stay
long after we are worn.

This bowl shines from hours of rubbing—
oil from the hand and grit.
This bowl sweats.

Fragments slip through our fingers.
The egret floats branch to branch
arrow-lengths ahead.
At night fog camps around the tent.
Stones are wet as severed hearts.
Dreams turn against stone,
over and over striking for fire.

What I do first
is dance the sacred songs.
When the song hooks,
I put down my mask
and go out on ice.

There is no one else.
No landmarks but memory,
the snow drifting
until I make it my house.

The hunt begins at the breath-hold
and I am the carving knife.

When the seal juts from the sea
and loops into sinew and bone
I thrust with my spear
and haul him up—

the first fresh food in months, blood
a warm spout down my throat.

How easy it is to forget
the long journey in,
the cold no skin can heat,
the light shifting out.

How easy to rest,
hours stretching days
into the zero of years.

I move to survive
the bear's hot breath
melting my tracks.

I move because hunger is ice,
it packs and drives.
Whatever lies in its path is crushed,
even those we love.

These are thoughts I bury in snow.
I know how easy it is
to play with souls of the dead
and be kept.

I hunt from need.
I hunt for blood
and fill my lamps with the oil of flesh.
I am the eater of raw meat,
hunger stored too deep to thaw.

..... from *Heartwood*

Once more we wait for the storyteller
to step into the margin and reveal intentions:
why the first letter flowered,
spiraling with intricate designs down the page.

Clues drop, mostly forgotten,
so on and so on stacked like bricks,
crumbling when we look back
a voice once close now a stranger.

All through the book we wild-guess the villain.
Deceived by this one or that,
we look for reprieve, a surprise ending,
the page turning to a house in the woods,
dogs locked up, gun put away.

In the still forest of words,
where the hidden appears in its season
hills darken and move in
Like lean horses that have rocked a long way home,
they circle the pool of our hands.
A deer riffles through leaves, then a bird
sings *begin again, begin again.*

Propped in his coffin,
my grandfather looked like the mummy of Seti I.

When my turn comes,
I want to die holding what I love,
the way windows catch as buildings rise
in a flare of sun.

Sometimes I wake trussed in my own arms,
the heart pressed down in its chest, smoldering.
Then I move to you, fumbling the body
as if it were possible to sink beyond pain
and surface forgetful of where we had been.

Morning, and the street rumbles through a day
like any other. Earth is peopling again
and we unfold, thirsty as lotus seeds
lifted from a tomb.

The year I traced over pictures in *Paradise Lost*,
mother complained. What she couldn't read
was the body I craved
pitched head-first and naked from heaven,
flesh and its rabble of feathers
an unquenchable fire.

Home from the hunt,
father dumped a rucksack of doves
on the kitchen table,
threw one still warm in my lap,
a dollop of blood crusted on its breast.

I fled, but soon crept back
to him sitting there, legs spread,
guts and feathers spiraling down
to mound at his feet,
a tiny wafer of lung lifted on the blade,
doves simmering in a pan
splashed with peppered wine.

Wrapped in fragrance,
I feasted that night and since.
Now I never see birds
without thinking how shamed they look
stripped, but how sinfully good
they go down—like Eve,
her belly, when she left the garden,
lusciously plumped.

You listen for a rap on the door,
the sister and brother you never had,
the mother who died too soon,
the father who drifted away,
and you set the table to put them in place.
Fork there, knife here—no,
wrong. You begin again,
rehearsing over and over
what you should have said, or will.

But hope sends regrets,
and when the cat slinks back, growling,
fur frizzed by shadows flickering outside,
you think of your throw-away child
who came too soon,
closing your father's mouth,
your mother's eyes.

The ghost still kicks under your heart.
And when an owl lands on the roof
and blows away, wind shuffling the leaves,
everything and nothing is the same.
You drift room to room plumping pillows
and picking up.
A last shivering look into the night
as you draw the curtains.
One by one the rooms go out.
Dark trees lean toward the house.
Limbs scratch the window panes.
You whisper, *come in.*

I

You know the wind is shifty
by the way clothes and hair
blow about in the gawking crowd.

The caption below reads,
The wire is life.
All the rest is just waiting around.

The man it quotes
walks a cable over a waterfall.

And why not—
Earth stands us only so long.

II

In another picture,
cypress trees are so perfectly
relayed to water,
you could turn the photo upside down
and say the real is only a reflection.

The foreground reeds are in sharper focus,
outer and mirrored halves
tied into neat bundles
by the waterline.

Calmed by such clarity,
you hardly notice the wavy line
that slides under
shadowing its own ripple.

Running from a loaded brush
the shore bleeds as color escapes.

III

The barn leans to one side,
pigeons in the loft,
boards scattered on the ground.

You can see through cracks
the way a dream is broken into
and gutted by light.

The house is no better,
the door hangs on one hinge,
the jamb blackened,
soot smeared over siding
like makeup left on overnight.

But the one intact window
in the back wing shines.
A luxurious plant smolders on the sill.
You know someone still lives there.

The way it was
when my father lay dying.
I talked to him for days
as if he could understand
and maybe he did, light flickering
in a small back room of his brain.

Let me see the spots on your lungs,
I ask my father.
Home from the sanitarium,
but not allowed to sit close,
he follows me with his eyes.
I am six years old, a show-off
whirling around his warmth.
He complains I need a winter coat.
Mother nods, smiles,
and whispers to the stove.
I flatten against the wall,
the year a cat's cradle
of delicate maneuvers,
my father the tangle.

He sings a bitter, off-key song,
Just around the corner
there's a rainbow in the sky,
and I believe
until the school bus veers into a dog,
and I watch a bloody spasm
smear the road, watch
a war they never thought would come
hit friends, my father muttering
I should have been called.

Afraid to look his way afraid not,
I fight and love in my own good time
remembering what he said.
If you lose the eye of a cornered fox,
it will disappear.

It stormed a lot that summer—
brute cloudbursts, pane-rattling thunder.
Open the front door and a bolt might rip
the length of a hall.

There were days of card games
and a battery of rain at the window.

The weeks racked up a list of disasters,
strikes on the golf course,
drownings by undertow.

A man on our block took to his boat
and never returned,
but the war took most,
bit by bit someone/no one we knew,
the way ants peel away from remains
hauling off piecemeal,
legs, thorax, wings.

We were left pin-on oak leaves and stars,
and a box of photos—a gallery
of uniformed figures in knocked out places
we could only conjure from books.

Villagers, flowers, ruddy cheeks—
what did we know?

Caught in the steady drizzle of our lives,
we hardly looked up from the game
of high-card-take-all.

Grandmother at the piano,
my father standing at her side,
lips a pursed line
violin pressed beneath his chin.

I find instrument and case
hidden in a corner of the attic,
strings flopping from the pegs,
a dent in the neck.

The day she died
he ran raging to his room
vowing never again to play—
threw case and all out the window.

A photograph shows the scar
where he beat his forehead on the floor.
Wait! I want to say,
my mother and I are coming.

He loved women,
told me I had a voice like his mother's,
so I chattered on and on while he found her shadow
in every woman he met, felt her touch
listening to Heifetz on the phonograph.

Accompanied by that sound
up and down as love's sweet moaning,
I circled the room
waiting for some note I was there,

the way my children circle me
with the same old tune,
You never listen to what I say.

My daughter wants the violin restrung,
wants lessons, nothing difficult, she adds
and I say yes to simple harmonies
we learn to pick up and put down.

You know how it is with young girls—
they wait to be carried off, bareback and wild,
feelings no longer corralled,
the field so fragrant
they blossom out of their own juice.

The first mounting hurt, but I held,
legs clamped to heaving sides,
a pounding beneath,
flanks lathered with froth.

And I was the one to break,
wouldn't have listened if told
how it is to hobble home
bruised and sore.

Once pain is born, it suckles us dry,
comes back unannounced,
racing for home, hungry for more.

There are times I ride from anger to tears,
at a loss where to go.

But I haven't run out.
Let one of them roll his eyes my way,
and I'm gone like before,
loving how they curve to bend down
and nuzzle, lips soft as challis,
warm breath cupped in my palms.

Leaning against the body,
I forget the times I was thrown.

Pull yours down first, he commands,
so I slip out of shorts and underpants
and spread my legs like he says.

Come on downstairs, his mother calls,
it's time to go home.

One last look and he runs
leaving me cheated out of my turn,
leaving me ashamed, yet wanting more
of the throb from his thumb's probe.
I sit for a while, listening
to the wall, as if there were an echo
I hadn't heard—kind words from him
that were stalled inside,
my mother's voice coming on strong.

What are you doing up there?

Picking up games, I say.

Good girl. Good girl.

On the vacant lot
At the corner of Dauphin and Broad,
they pitched a tent, sent out the call

REVIVAL
COME MEET YOUR SAVIOR

We could depend on
Amen there, Brother!
a lot of rolling in the aisles
and talking in tongues.
Best of all, Bible stories acted out.

Trash! our Episcopal parents scorned.
Not us. We sneaked in under the tent flap,
down on our knees in mud and sin,
and between the preaching and scenes,
when they passed the plate,
we ducked out, then in again.

The last time under,
John Mac put his hand on my thigh
and rubbed on up.

Tumbling onto the fresh crushed clover,
I craved what I felt.
    Amen, Sister!
sang out for the Second Coming
                                    sang

O perfect love—
    the wafer melting on the tongue,
    that fountain filled with blood—
                            love,

an everlasting thirst,
the well deep where we came to draw.

From the house, lamp-light on snow.
This is you looking at me,
says the child,
showing the drawing
of a face at the window.

His voice clatters on and on,
and you pay no attention
until it quiets.
Then you stop and listen,
the way a dog pricks up its ears
and bristles
at something felt
down the walls of its gut.

Bitten by cold,
you're driven in,
the story of your life
stacked on the hearth.

The memory held of home,
a child's glass globe,
a house flurried with snow—

snow, a fall of white roses
over the fence,
the fence sloughing its load
the way a child's face
spills what it can't contain.

Tell me a story he says,
and wants it word for word the same,
beginning to end.
Holding his hand, I sit by the bed,
light from the hall splattered across his face
as I talk about the old barn, the club
where I crossed my heart and hoped to die
for vows and names written in blood.

I tell how scissors were made
by crossing pins on the trolley rail,
how I swung on pines whipped down so deep
my hair swept the ground,
and I tell how the warmth of milk toast
puddled with butter, forgave all fevers.

I let pass the nights I've cried out in deliriums,
as if tears could quench the fires
that leave me poking through ash,
let pass the clutch of cottonmouth snakes
knotted at the bottom of the creek.

I tell how it was to dive
in the black, sun-silvered water,
then rise in a seltzer of breath.

Why should he know how we go down
unfinished, arms flailing, voice pleading,
Hold me, pull me out.

Portraits in the front hall
were painted to stare straight on
no matter where we stood.
My mother, small: her hair, smoke.
Out on the porch
she rocks on father's lap.
I watch with a catch in my throat
as he murmurs in her ear.
She goes to the hospital,
and I bury a doll, a ring,
a collection of shells.
Summer is long,
night after sweltering night
the far-off plea
of a chuck-will's-widow
deep in the swamp.
Worse than counting sheep,
that harangue haunting the room
where I sprawl like driftwood,
my sweaty sleep interrupted
by the *will will* of a bird
drilling to nerve.
The screen door slams,
mother returns to lie by the window.
Sometimes I interrupt play to wave.
Father brings her his prize camellias—
variegated pinks, fleshy reds
and maroons, smoldering on a tray.
The nurse sings
Sweet Little Jesus Boy.
I count on will to sleep, but walls are thin,
I hear my father pacing his room.

I've got Iceland! my father shouts
and fits the earphones to my head.
I hear static, a voice that comes and goes.

Close, yet so far, he whispers to mother
as she lolls back in his arms.
This is one of his rare days home
from the sanitarium.
He swats me gently out of the room.
Left to dolls, I listen in.

Murmurs fade into walls,
into a school where nuns
taught me to say bonjour, bonsoir,
though I could never remember
to match the time of day.
Reversals had to do
with my father's come and go.

Window-shopping, mother and I
stepped around men
sprawled in transient spaces
where the wind blew least.

A mug of cocoa and buttered toast
was all I had or wanted for lunch.
I wasn't as hungry then,
didn't scrape the plate of every crumb,
didn't hear the cold wind
loaded with voice,
or feel its breath ghosting my father,
hanging on as I did, then and now.

I once had a friend
whose family let peacocks stroll in the yard.
When we played on the porch,
they flew to the roof and looked down,
necks curved in a sidewise U over eaves,
heads twisting from eye to eye
for a better view.

Hearts and Monopoly were favorite games.
Above, the cock rattled his feathers and stomped
while the peahen pecked at tile.

At night I could hear them scream blocks away.
Their love song, but to us the cry of a wounded child
stumbling through rubble.

Spread like a color wheel, the peacock's tail
grounds an eye in the storm of each feather.
If all the eyes covering our lives were to open,
they would terrify.

I keep a jar of feathers in the house.
Bad luck, some say.
The fringe of a feather trembles
at the slightest change of air.

Step on a crack,
break your mother's back.
I watch my cat jerk to death
screaming under the wheels of my car.
Not your fault, the family commiserate,
but I know better—
the moment we go slack
a piece of the world comes to harm.
No dodging the parts rushing out.
Some rev up to the speed of light,
or unthinkably faster.
We could look up one night
and see the sky totaled,
a wreck beyond salvage.
Buried beneath all that rubble,
our wake is an unsteady sleep-walk at best.
Earth grinds its teeth, basins tremble,
east and west tear apart.
We dream the land whole again,
no longer a puzzle,
but eventually the wish jumbles.
Last night a dog or fox
dug into the cat's backyard grave.
Today I fill the shaft
with gravel, stones, bricks—
whatever I've trashed.

I envy sleepers.
Days my grandfather worked in the yard,
he would lie on the grass and nap.
Think how few sleep
in that gentle position,
ankles crossed, hands clasped over chest.

He died asking for me, but I wasn't there.
No good reason why.
These pages wait to catch my lies,
so I collect masks: the one from New Guinea
with tongue hanging out means go away.

I mean stay. Walk the floor with me
and I'll tell you about the many
who rapped on my window too late.

Certain as a cocked gun,
a saffron-robed man runs up to my car
and flashes a charm.
Look, he says, *soul*,
and I want to believe.
but halfway home we could be blown
through a hole in an egg.

I dream otherwise,
dream the ones wasting away
are not too far gone to retrieve.
I've keened too long over shreds of flesh.
Tell me the dead sleep whole and warm.
Tell me I'm not in their nightmares.

Toward the end,
rarely more than whispers,
the tumor on your brain
packed around words
that wander in and out.

The room dimmed by blinds
and an alley brick wall,
my aimless chatter
rambling like a child
who won't sit still.

You, my father,
staring over me
at a bawling soap opera
as I lift your hand,
clean the nails,
and push back cuticles
that reveal bruised
half-moons.

Too late for help,
the nurse brings medicine
we encourage you to drink.

Look at me.

Pulling back your hand,
you wave at needling shadows
flicked across TV,
the words I want to say,
static in my mouth.

A winter so cold
windows are glazed inside.

The house
a beast crouched to leap.

At night the yellow panes
reflect flickering light

ancient as first fires,
the ghosts of parents drifting

through the faces of children
clustered at the window

chattering
as they scratch on glass,

their names melting
in the wake of their nails.

Adam and God finger the space
between them as if to connect
the dome to everlasting.

Not my child
who slipped off unfinished,
the one who never sucked breath,
the one who swam
from darkness to drowning.

In that resonant silence
that deepens, may he rock
gently toward light.
May the child wedged in stone
at the bottom of a well
keep until the tunnel connects.

Sometimes at night
I hear my husband's voice
catch, and hang for one,
two, three and more counts
before I shake him to life,

and finally dreams
that allow us anything, everything,
without matter.

I want to put my feet down
without the crackle of dead leaves—
dogwood, sumac, and maple bled grey.

Hidden in the body's dark wood,
a beast circles fire.
Wants to go, wants to stay.

I jab at embers that burn to ash,
a thin streak of smoke trespassing sky,
wind coming on fast.

*...the curious relation between one fragment
of nature and another which all the same explain
and enhance each other...*

I

Red is the color I love, the body's flower,
a stalk lifting, petals opened
to a deeper violet so mortally sweet we forget
how soon the season storms us down.

Days when trees black-whip the sky,
we are cleansed by the sadness of rain,
sun pulsing back, gold rippling the air,
the field revealing shards and arrowheads.

Once I stood under the stars
and wished my life would hold right there—
wouldn't have listened if told
the heart is loaded to turn on itself.

But I can defend what wounds me.
When mauve tumors bloomed on my father's brain,
I pictured him young again, the patches of memory
a field crossing an immense plain,
in repose, a vague consonance of colors
stroked by the wind to quiver and rise
like green, yellow, and ocher wheat.

II

I fill my mother's silhouette,
the eyes she didn't pass on,
the stubs of lashes she cut as a child
sure they would grow in long.

Kneeling, she digs a hole,
wets it down with moss and flowerets
then covers the miniature grotto
with a broken piece of glass.

The flowers will wilt, I complain.
Wait, she says, you'll see.
The next morning daisy, rue, and anemone
stretch upwards as if freshly clipped,
sun flashing off limpets of moisture
clinging to the underside of glass.

III

A day clear as watercolor
washes into night and the color of fear,
and I am the child
with a sheet pulled over her head,
afraid of creaking floors,
afraid doors and windows will open on black.

IV

Time buzzes around us, bottle-green,
and we are so ripe.
A man places his easel against a haystack,
and shoots himself, grazing the heart.

On the walls of the room where he lies,
all the last canvases are nailed,
forming something of a halo,
sunflowers, dahlias, daisies,
the day so made for him
he could still be riffling wheat,
or deepening the sky at horizon-line.

He is the tilted crow screaming at the wind,
the storm about to break.

Death is a deep Prussian blue
swirled by the stars,
our colors cross-hatched in space—
wild flowers seared by flames,
ash drifting for a landing place.

..... from *The Angel of Obsession*

I hear them before they come into sight
clipping a swath of mist
as they move diagonally across
sweet-gum and oak, the call
poignant as a night train
approaching half-sleep,
the dream it interrupts, here and gone,
fading into the dark.
A kind of bruise we find on the body,
not remembering what brought it about.

It amuses me to imagine what is beyond a hill. I want so much
to represent those things I will never see.
Yves Tanguy

Above the spire across the street,
stars float like bell notes,
high, low, a clash of meteorites
scattering acids in space,
perhaps the people we've yet to meet,
not here but in another oasis.
Think how close we are.
I once found a fluted stone in a field.
The blade felt right to my hand
as if I had notched the sides
and thrown the shaft. But "why"
is a slippery dune hard to mount
without tumbling, answers often gritty.
If there were an ocean on the other side,
imagine sailing to a land peopled
with those we love and want back, or—
admit it—someone unknown,
the one we've looked for all our lives,
the one we'd sacrifice others to meet.
The bank of clouds on the horizon,
now black, now gray, a silhouette
of hills and trees gradually filled
with the primaries—blood, bile,
the grief of blue,
and rushing to the foreground,
a commotion, a tease of randomness
that kinks the world we imagine
waving us into its arms.

Pale and unplucked, Eve kneels in the left panel,
her heart not yet driven to wander.
I envy the angels who fell around her.
In that dawn, fumbling naked and warm
to a mass of tattered wings,
did they tongue one another's wounds

and by that innocent act discover
how the body moves, how the hand,
fingering plush skin, divines
an underground river,
its caverns and whispers?

As animals begin to devour each other,
the sour taste of blood draws them back
again and again to lap from its pool.

It's the middle scene that excites us,
the carnal indifference,
the exotic sport of catch-as-catch-can.

But in the final panel the world comes true,
sky exploding like a rotten fruit,
the landscape filled with the clatter of machines.
Cones of light lash over craters
where the wounded lie, skewered,
wings covered with ash,
their dreams rubble.

And there in the left foreground,
like children lost in a mob,
you and I face outwards, as if for rescue.
Urgent now, you lean on my breast,
our tongues desperate from the heart's Babel.

Like an ancient bend
reclaimed by the river,
the absence of fear
is filled with its own memory:

the time you were carried
trembling up steps to a landing
to wait out a storm,
your mother soothing you

with stories, her hold serene
as Giorgione's Madonna
who nurses her child
against a raging background,

the muted facade of a town
flashed into life,
clouds thundering gray-green
across what seems no end

of a night torn by lightning.
Your mother's face illumined
as you lean to her warmth,
even then slight, and cooling

as the seconds shut down.
The stairwell, a darkness
you imagine pouring
through windows and doors

that won't close, your feet
mired as time thunders closer
chasing you back into nightmares
that sometimes woke true.

You, the loss of all you've owned,
recover the memory of mother
and child as if coming home,
as if love lies

where you always pictured it,
in the calm of the storm.
Even when love lies,
it's the dream you cling to.

Today drifts into yesterday.
Difficult to remember
the food eaten, rooms cleaned.

Same with books, you read,
read, but recall only
that someone floated off,

finally, from years of solitude,
and danced naked in a bowler hat.
The nose has a better memory,

whole lives waft back, the moments
that linger in limbo
pulled out by a random scent.

And you stand in the street
watching a cab drive off
leaving in its wake

the aroma of a man's cigarette
that even now revives
the way his fingers pressed

hard into your thigh,
the hairs on his wrist
suddenly stricken with sunlight.

Memory, the ruins of experience.
Mark Stevens

Yes, I remember
the French clock on the mantel,
the boat on top rocking the minutes away.
No, said my maiden aunt,
not even when she was young
did it run, maybe years before.

In eterno...in eterno...
Mahler ends his song,
and leaves us wondering
how much the earth sustains,
how much is tossed
or left unsung.
When my aunt died
I threw away her letters
hidden in an attic trunk.

Dear Augusta, I'm sorry
it had to end like this,
causing such anguish,
but you were the one
who refused to leave
your father and the house.
Forgive me.
I will always...

I burn more than I save,
but a dress in the attic
drags up dust—
a child talking to herself,
like a dialogue between keys
and strings, so resonant
we forget its solo.

Your last note to me...
your tears, so beautiful...
I'll never forget...

I had forgotten,
but not those shed an hour ago.

When I say I love you, believe
for the moment it's true.
We're born possessed,
the closet emptied
and crammed again,
books opened to the pages
we live over and over,
the clock winding down
on the plot.

I did what a child dares,
threw a thermometer on bathroom tile
to scatter mercury,
then with the tip of a finger
tapped the droplets into a kindred pool.

I see myself in each of my children.
Where are we headed, I want to know.
Not that I'm afraid of turns
or unmarked routes—
it's the going too fast.

Watch out, I caution,
and step into space from stairs.

A man crosses the street to help me up.
We exchange names and numbers
before falling back on our ways,
odds and ends left jingling
in the pocket of the other's life.

Quicksilver, that sometime-messenger,
sometime-thief.

Rummaging through the attic,
the children find a violin
that belonged to my father.
I draw the bow across strings
and we take turns pulling out sound,

notes flying off *spiritus mercurius,*
talk scattering between us
until time to go.

They wave goodbye and drive off
the risk of mishap carried along.
Possibilities too—the alchemy of love
returning its vapors transformed:
a look, a voice, a touch,
glistening before me.

The children accuse me
of saying one thing meaning another.
I wake up complaining to the dark:
so what, if truth sleeps in twin beds,
that's no cause for divorce.

Falling back to sleep,
I make promises I know I'll break.
In the morning, familiar aromas
of shaving cream and toast,
the sun pooled in a cup of tea.

News on television flashes
from scene to scene—arms laid down,
in a square, thousands of jubilant shouts,
the air so cold breath hovers
like a cartoon balloon
filled with simple words,
no double-talk.

Only the old, bundled in memory, weep
and wait for tanks to rumble
from a cornered street
toward a soft sprawl of bodies—
the sons and daughters we love to death.

I turn savage with my children.
Wake up, I demand,
you've slept long enough.

And I make New Year promises,
including a few I'm sure to keep:
I will die,
I will take my memories with me,
I will leave survivors tossing in theirs.

There are nights I fight sleep,
dizzy sometimes with success,
my dreams left lusting for more.

Don't get me wrong,
I love the easy seductions,
the costumes and masks,
the garbled lines,
one person merging into another.

But the play moves on,
scrambling scenes in the darkness,
no one answering cues.

Same as those faces
we see on the evening news,
children dying in roles
they haven't rehearsed.

Mama, they're killing me!
Rufina Amalya hears her son scream.
Somewhere in the carnage
her husband sprawled dead.

And there the dialogue ends,
but the cries follow us,
follow all day and into our sleep,
assuming the nightmare.

Too much for this woman
in the front row.
Not even an *Excuse me*
when she crashes out.

Fast as we build roads
between the cities of want and have,
monsters fall out of rock.
Tracks, trails, bones, teeth,
impressions on shale—
pieces of a jumbled puzzle.

Not knowing what to expect,
we collect fossils, tame them
on tables and shelves,
stack them in gardens,
border the walks.

Examining the fine print of dendrites
which look like fossils but aren't,
I think how figments gull us into belief,
while the real brute lurks
to break out of shadow.

And what of the first, delicate,
small-frame bones—
who would have expected *tyrannos*?

If you were to find me limed in stone,
a vestige of silk outlining my skeleton,
beads scattered about,
would you wonder about the axe in my hand?

Twenty-foot python found living under house in Orlando

He thought the racket that morning
was from cats, until he looked out
in time to see a coon swallowed headfirst,
feet kicking to the last.

The snake must have crawled
the neighborhood at night to feed.
You'd think someone driving home late
would have seen it sliding
across the road.

Maybe lovers parked under the oak
could sense how close danger looped,
a breath caressing the neck,
a stroke down the back.

"Lock your doors!"
every mother cries,
knowing how love
can squeeze us to death.

Thought of that crawl space
chills—the cold fixed eyes,
the heat-seeking pit,
the hiss of the furnace as it blows
the darkness into our lives.

The woman steps down from the bus
into a swarm of paparazzi,
a new dress boxed under her arm,
not a cloud smearing the sky.
She has yet to learn
her children and husband are dead.
Murder. Suicide.

Story after story, the same
sun-baked day,
muted guns at the border,
women berry picking in a field near town.
I gave my love a willow sprig, they sing.
A few kilometers away, the enemy
slips through the forest.

Say happiness is suspect,
reason enough to knock on wood
before the axe swings.
Barbed questions catch us
trying to escape.
Were the women left sprawled
across rows of blood?
Were the children asleep
when the father raised his gun?

Say we're incapable of certain acts.
Say it again.

Boxcars rattle through the countryside,
crammed with the fear
that this is not just a change of camps.
The pitch night swells with screams,
the ground between trees
strewn with owl pellets,
those indigestible remains
of lives swallowed whole.

An owl hoots from a nearby tree.
A siren floats off down the street.
Lying here covered by the warm night,
I don't want to think of torn flesh.

Once while we slept,
your fingers dug into my thigh.
I was bruised for days.

So tender are we to touch,
the body reacts without knowledge,
not because of it,
mumbling along even as we die,
the way an animal brought down
continues to kick
while a spasm of guts spirals out.

Don't tell me that old wives' tale
about the owl call, not now.
The moon rests like a benediction
on the bed where we sprawl
exhausted by love.

I

El Salvador, 1978

The day ends like this:
he slams the bolt on their screams,
washes gore from his hands,
and orders his driver
to help with his boots. At home,
his wife meets him in the foyer.
He slides one hand up and down her back,
the other massages her breasts.
They go upstairs.
You could say he's efficient.

II

Hamburg, 1934

Hours go by,
we lie on our backs
as if buried alive.
The sound of boots.
Men searching the house.
The floor overhead shakes.
I imagine him lifting the boards,
a smile on his face as he kneels
to stroke my cheek
with the barrel of his gun.
Open your mouth, he commands.

III

Argentina, 1977

Pain is an echo
that screams back
higher, higher.
In time I'm numbed
by the unspeakable things they do—
nine men—but I tell nothing,
have nothing to tell, except
that you and I are friends—
you, my once-lover, love
a word I no longer know,
its exquisite tortures aborted.

IV

Warsaw, 1944

Some things we escape,
but it's impossible
to rub from sight
the truckloads—men, women,
children—lined up and shot
ka puck ka puck,
then kicked into a ditch,
their eyes gouged out.
Is it because the dead
have a way of staring through us
I still hear the cries?

V

Is it because we are taught
turn the one cheek,
then the other—
it could be an angel you meet—
that we are willing to plead,
yes, yes there is reprieve,
only at the last
slipping our arms
into death's frayed sleeves?

I could be anywhere in the States.
The train, a local, kids in jeans,
scrubby towns strung between stations.
Only the red-tiled roofs
and confusion of language seem out of place.
Then Chartres, perched on its hill,
wings pressed against walls
that hold other walls from tumbling,
the town sprawled at the base.

And I'm on my knees at the sight.
The mutation of stone into glass—
sapphire, rose, chrysoprase—
a kaleidoscope of slivers
held in the middle of a turn.

To think that a manic order
could bring it to ruin.

The poor still give alms
and the sick are no better,
but the saints look humanly down
as if, at this moment,
they had stepped to the porch for air.
No matter that they crumble.
The lamp is on the nail.
Nothing much changed,
only the more impossible ways we die,
not these stones, the rapture,
rising for now out of our hands.

From a painting by Antonello da Messina

Hers isn't the usual
cherubic face.
This angel looks used,
as if she's been around
long enough to call
sorrow her home,
as if, street-wise,
nothing up to now
could ruffle her.

Wings tell the story,
the plumage buzzard-black,
a streak of crimson
on the folds.

The crucified body,
propped against her shoulder,
is strung with clotted blood
from a gash under his breast,
mouth slack, eyes slit
to indifference.

As she leans forward
to catch the backward thrust,
one arm twines around his,
her face turned to us
so that we get the full impact
of those unexpected tears.

The ground around them
is strewn with grave-spill,
skulls, bones, without name.
In the far distance,
a few figures mill
around a cross.

The angel's sorrow is utter.
She seems to know something
we don't but the body
is too heavy for her to lift.
Even if she could,
where would they go?

The first bird chirps into dawn
as if all the sounds ever made
had hardened there.

Even now someone is crying
and we won't hear.

I turn to your side of the bed,
but you wander off in a dream,
that haven where the body can let go
and not care if we fall,
disaster flicked off so lightly
you might think it an eyelash,
the dream blinking on despite the loss.

It's morning we suffer—
in and out of arms,
now they lay us down, here,
grounded in blood.
So sleep...
there is still time
before the one last star
explodes into day,
time before the nightmare cry
comes aloud.

Half awake, I stand on the doorstep,
ink on the morning paper still damp,
my hands smearing the words.

Some of us go to bed scared,
Einstein for one, afraid
if he slept he would fall through.

Perhaps he forgot how the girl in the fairy tale
fell down the well of her dreams
into the arms of a prince
who held her ever after
from milking cows.

Maybe he thought of the man
who walked in his sleep, yelled
                    Thief!
and shot his wife.

Dreams confuse, have energy without mass,
a jumbled equation scrawled on a blackboard
erased at sunrise.

A friend calls, threatening her life.
Her nightmare is the mouth emptied of words.

What I fear most is seeing the night through.
Not the dream, but its grotesque tatter
flapping at day.

I once saw a man force his child
to the window of a wrecked car,
hold the boy's head over the dead
and shout, Look! Look!

I change beds, roam the house, read
the mind is charted into hemispheres,
some oriented left, others right.

The day is touch as touch can,
but the dream is a reflection on multiple mirrors,
no end to the depth.
it is the scent haunting a forgotten room,
a door that opens on the dead,
the countless unborn,
and the few we ever really knew.
It is the love we live for a time,
and the hate—guiltless, true.

Don't tell me the dream you've had
time and again,
the nightmare that fails to catch you
flying, luckily, above it all,
your body jerked up before it lands
sound awake in bed,
the mound a pillow not a grave,
teeth, bones, flesh intact,
the warm breath sleeping next to you,
the one constant.
Don't tell me.
For every dream like that,
another splatters rock-bottom,
refusing to evaporate.
Don't tell me how we run
slow-motion to escape,
the ground an escalator
winding the opposite way—or worse,
the road we arrive on
going even as we come.
Don't tell me the people we meet
flip from face to face.
I believe what I dream.
When the train on the other rail
slides back and leaves
an illusion of moving forward,
I ride that.
Don't tell me the face at the window
is only reflection,

a life conjured
the moment it flashes by.
Don't tell me it was my mouth
pressed against glass.
Don't tell me the mouth is a dream.

.....*Dreaming the Dead*

*All who leave the earth go to the moon which is swollen
by their breath during the first half of the month.*
from the Upanishads

That's when the moon gives us hell,
dogs in the neighborhood crouched in a howl,
the dead all talking at once.
you'd think there were better things to do
than loll around in dreams,
but the dead don't mind, they can't wait
to be called under sheets where we sprawl
with our gowns hiked up, can't wait
to dump their grievances.
And when we close in with excuses,
they give us the brush-off.

Writing down what was done or said
won't recover the plot as it was.
Fitful faces dissolve and remake,
luring us again through scene after scene,
the moon tugging, desire waxing.
Tonight I wished on a shooting star,
but the kettle whistles for tea,
and the cry of a wakeful child
demands a story that turns on light.
These are our saviors
when the moon spins us foolish.

I think of the wishes I made
and how lucky I am so few came home.

The sound of rain purls around us—
curve, hollow, all the retreats we fish in—
the world a far-off thunder in the mountain,
not twisted bodies swept down-stream.

We float off to sleep in a tangle of limbs,
the bed an ark filled with our beasts,
the dream more than once flying out
in search of a landing place.

Rain rails against the window panes
as if its life depended on us to open up.
The words *I love you* pour, then a drought
until the next deluge greens.
Before water runs bitter,
there is a lake back in the hills
so clear you would hope a hunter,
dropping to rest, would look at his bloody hands
and decide *no, not here.*

Here we lie like any two rivers that come
together with casualties piled in our wake.
For a time we soothe one another and forgive
how easily the wanted are drowned.

Pummeling the land, rain softens the dead.
In retreat, it smears a stain across the ceiling
above our bed. Even now you drift away.

In the darkness a mist hovers close
and you wake damp with longing.

It's the angel of dreams,
the one who leaves you undone,
a scent of sex in the air,
the feckless shadows fading.

All you remember is a delicious
tongue probing your ear.

That's why the angel of no-nonsense
demands day. It's the one
who stares into your eyes
during moments so intimate or cruel
you look the other way.

Isn't this what you wanted?
Honesty? Undivided attention?

When night comes back to roost,
pinions swoop down
raking your flesh.

You're captive
to a persistent harangue
like that from a willful child
banging a piano.

The angel of obsession
drags its wings on the ground,

and you follow,
indifferent to those left
calling your name.

We graze on the edge of sleep.
Far off the lowing of a train.
You pull me closer as if I might leave,
the sound lulling us into a kind of slumber
of where we've been, or want to be.

Once when we came to a stop,
I lifted the shade to my berth
and a man from another life stared back
waiting to take your place.

Sleek and oiled, trains slide into stations
where Indians hold up beads,
their faces an empty plain.
And I'm the child on the bike,
waving at arrivals I dream will be mine.

Gone, in a trail of smoke. The dead,
the dying—all who leave—sleepers
rattling back and forth.

Miles seem to slow
when we look into the distance
where mountains anchor oceans
and ancient fires—

and the past we'd like to excavate,
playing the stories over, this time
on cue, filling in the people we missed,
the terminus we never reached,
the train pouring back into our lives.

Maple buds break red to mingle
with the Judas trees now purpling.
The betrayer is my heart,
March taking its airs from rain
to soften towards April,
another year pulling me along.

So much goes unrevealed,
tombs ransacked, names effaced.
When I climbed the final passageway
into Cheops' burial chamber, there,
high on the wall, was the name Belzoni,
nothing of who he was.

Also silent: hands outlined in caves,
hands we continue to clutch,
and let fall for other hands, hands
stroking as if that tracery would beget
its own gallery of echoes.

This morning I passed a sign:
SISTER LEISHA TELLS YOUR FUTURE
AND PAST.
But I haven't the time.

It's Arbor Day, the day
they give away seedlings
of Buckeye, Peach, and River Birch.
Time again for rooting blind,
the year's bitter pit, succulent flesh.

I don't want the chiseled slab
with name and date fading to gray,
I want the angel in the old cemetery,
the classy one whose wings are fluffed
and right leg flexed
as if about to take off,
the one who all these years
tried to whisper in my ear as I ran by
with plastic flowers in my arms.

I want to lie down stripped
under its weight,
my hands no longer fists,
its breath grazing my flesh—

me, the one who falls into my life
thinking, sure, I can fix up the place,
but bones expose themselves
despite perpetual care, and the mole gouges,
snout and claws finding me out.

I want to rise,
hanging on for dear, dear life,
the way I rode shoulders
when I was a child,
want to step out into a jungle
of temples lost in people
we're bound to stumble across,

my angel and I singing together
in a crazy off-key way,

my angel with chipped nose,
and bird shit on its wings.

Listen, one says but the other doesn't

The usual
Shouting over a great distance
Static the answer

Or the long silence of a bottle
bobbing on the ocean

If it were possible
To gather all the wasted words
Which would I keep
Which would keep you

I bump into the warm stall of your body
Yes I love you yesyes

Words can take or leave gravity
I like to think they graze between stars

Mine yours
In a dumb way close
Until a tongue calls them home

for Guy Owen

The path isn't responsible.
Wandering off, it sometimes splits,
or ends at briar patch and field,
like the trail I took today
following the mountain's foot.

Did the first ones to find this place
stand and stare across blue-eyed grass
and huckleberry bush,
the path broken, abandoned
to thin lines running off at random
like pottery-craze?

What is it about this clearing
that scatters us—
each lost in the self swallowed
by the dark implosion of leaves,
or drawn to the glitter of mica,
galaxy after galaxy
embedded in the cold range
out of reach until stone crumbles
and light drifts.

I put my foot in your step.
and our bodies pick up the same dust.
Rising, settling to rise again,
it is a permanence impossible to shake
once we enter its universe.

Walk around St. Catherine's Hill
and you'll see the sides ribbed
with reminders of an Iron Age fort,
the slopes not so far away as they seem
from ducks and geese
riffling the meadow streams.

It's possible to recall a whole life
from remains, a ship from nailheads
and imprints, those who sailed
showing up like refugees
worn from centuries of storm.

High on a ledge
of Winchester Cathedral,
the bones of Canute and his queen
lie jumbled in a casket.
An intimate disorder.

One text of the Bible
opens on an unfinished page
of roughed-in figures the eye fills
with colors of its own choosing.
Words are gold illuminating the hours.

Mead spilled from lip into song
from this silver flagon traded across water.

In late afternoon when shadows
overflow, our communion with the past
breaking the day, you can almost believe
walls still ring the mound,

reflections dropping into a pool
where they shatter
in the wake of a black swan
before rushing back whole.

The poem about Greece refuses to end.
It runs on like a water color, blending
the way sky and sea touch and let go,

from time to time flooding our lives
as if the gods still spoke
and we understood.

Diving in, we bring up fragments.
A hand matches an arm, stones engage,
the vase holds.

In the temple, a crazy old woman
babbles for translation.

Again we're thrown into a sea
that holds us buoyant
so long as we breathe,

a panic of fish scattering,
blue-green turning up bronze and gold.

My stay here goes forward, which is not to say
I am anywhere near finishing.
Claude Monet

I

Days drift by,
and the farther away we stand,
the clearer they reflect
layer over layer of flowers, trees, shrubs,
mirrored on water, wisteria so purple-plumped
it spills, and colors continue to pour,
what can't be seen
moving under the surface.

Grass sways at the bottom of a pond,
a quiver of stalks splays into lilies,
lilies floating tethered,
the way a long-submerged memory
floats up,
      surprised
by a furious shower of light.

II

Light travels through space like an ice-crack
splintering when it hits.
We swim into color, flushed,
someone there to stroke us into shape.

When the wobbling head of my son
broke those waters, the wet
warm smack of his mouth startled
runnels of milk down my breast.

The heart pumps out, and I forget
how the tide leaves us strewn,
the planet shunting its crust.

III

To slow our drop into darkness,
I sleep holding on to you,

and dig into the body as if for a gem
that would keep the rest of our lives unflawed,
dig until the voice cries out in a tongue
we speak but rarely understand.

Maybe one day we'll strike a vein
filled with crystals,
and find ourselves waiting to be born
red, gold, black, for once transparent,
held in a flash-fire face to face with love.

IV

Racing away with our memories,
the galaxies recede in all directions.
The older I become,
the farther back I reflect
on those I first held close.

There, in the milky way of childhood,
I ride on my father's shoulders
to watch a parade, the night torch-lit,
figures flickering by in costumes and masks.

You lie nearer, but what do we really know
of ourselves. When you hold me
I'm lost, the body darting off like a child.

V

A million years ago,
fire slumbered among hammer stones,
chips, pieces of bone.

A woman runs and falls by the shores
of a lake, gets up, falls again to stay
covered by volcanic ash, the remains
emptied, only an outline left to recall.

But the dead continue to root:
a profusion of graves, those raped,
or shot, covered with leaves
the wind brushes through.

Upstairs in dreams,
we ignore the creaking floors.
A log shifts
and a shower of sparks hits the hearth.
You murmur, turn,
and we drop back to sleep,
the rug left smoldering.

VI

Nightmares sometimes repeat,
but with variations so that we can say
     It won't be like this next time.
Next time we move in,
again on the same fault line.

VII

The moon bobs free from a stroke of cloud,
one side plucked off, the next night thinner
and thinner, until only a petal remains,

but enough that we continue to believe
in making a slow way back,
whole as before.

VIII

You surface in every face,
so close I feel the life once lived—
a wilderness cluttered with remains,
the planet wasting us age to age,
our changes like weather on radar.

When you come,
the hairs on my thighs rise
like grass after rain.

Once more to taste your tongue,
the words you leave in my mouth.

And after the sweet sloughing of flesh,
and gradual descent through fault and stress,
the bones of memory click in place
reconstructing what we lost—
a revenant come home.
I have loved you all my lives.

..... from *The Dark Takes Aim*

Three a.m., the house a foreign country I wake in,
same language but a different inflection,
a creak on the stair a harbinger,
the jolt into insomnia an alert.

In an etching by Goya, demons perch on a bedpost
and clamor for the sleeper's heart.

Long ago we knelt for prayers
but those children have slept for years,
dream merging child into beast.
       Somewhere
a truck explodes and bodies bloom
with fleshy extravagance of peonies—
         forgive me,
not petals but a scream settling on entrails,
bone, meat, our betrayals piling in gutters.

It should be obvious where the fault lies,
yet we continue to build there, the structure
collapsing into itself, the century in ruins.
       Somewhere
a trail remains, linking our inlands,
the path to summers in the mountains
where a halo of hummingbirds
crowns the feeder,
rock hectored by a snow-fed river,
mist from the falls beading our hair.

Moving as we do from the body
and its parochial demands to lessons of love,
you might say we succeed as often as not,
on call even as we sleep.

                           Even as we sleep,
the cry of a puma cracks the night.

At a distance:
seemingly intact piers,
dark recesses, blind arcades.

Nearer, the sky
pours through arches,
a drizzle of rain inside the nave,
the passage crumbling,
open to grass and grazing sheep.

On good days
strokes of sun the trespasser,
devastation given a kind of splendor,

the strobe lights of memory
playing out impressions of a tower
you know is not there,

nor are the bells,
nor the stalls, nor choir,
not one finger tapping time
on the carved arms of chairs
or intertwined

here the church,
here the steeple,
open the door

no vaulting hosannas, the chalice
and wine of remembrance
long removed,

as were the tapestries,
as was the incense of flesh
not yet carrion, not yet stringing off
into sorrow, base silence.

When I held my first son,
how perfect he seemed.
Driving home late,
we would sing rounds
O how lovely is the evening
his head nodding to my lap.

Blessings on that third
of our lives spent in sleep,
the plots of the day
left dangling.

Once I drove by a woman
clinging to a viaduct's ledge,
police, priest, and the curious
crowded below, the road
curving past into a benign
vista of cows and trees.

Blessings on those moments of reprieve
grabbed before dropping into nightmare.

How could my son fracture,
unaware of the split?
Ominous, the day I waited
on his porch, cake in hand
as if food could assuage
a mind reeling off.

Get out! Get out! The door slammed.
What I dread is a stand-off,
barricades, guns, police
with no choice but to shoot.

Blessings on the daughter
who ripens with a life
that turns us around again,
this time, we hope,
the helix of notes
descending in tune.

For a while we let pass
what Aeschylus said,
how at night
the pain that can't forget
falls drop by drop
upon the heart.

The moon floats off,
the dog whimpers under the steps.
How lovely the evening
with a child on my lap,
a circle of us singing
heedless of the dark taking aim.

What we knew we didn't know,
recalling only the threat of ice,
a hint of rain, or a dip
in the pool of desire.

As in childbirth, there was pain,
pain that no longer pounds
as it did yesterday,
blood drying under blood.

God gives us only what we can bear.
Is that so? whisper the dismembered,
their bones unable to stroke
the body to a shimmer.

In Siberia, a woman still fleshed
is lifted frozen from a crypt,
her limbs tattooed with whorls
of brilliant blue—a menagerie
of exotic beasts.
One of her long tapered
fingers points as if to touch.

From the headdress and adornments—
possibly a priestess. Holy,
the way she is carried overhead
on a canvas bier to the plane, to the lab
where her body will be plundered.

Such probes leave us wanting,
tell us little of those who broke away,
now scattered who knows where—
beautiful fragments
we may never recover.

We've heard the story:
his young wife bleeds
for the child born dead.
Sitting out the night
he leans into the lament,
left foot propped,
legs spread
under the guitar in his arms.
The woman kneels
in that shadowy space
between, his hand
stroking the dark plunge
of hair to breasts,
his hand swooning
over the chords,
one finger pressed there,
another here, probing
the body's thrum,
the audience a held
breath away.
Lay a hand over the heart
and feel it pump, a flow
tuned to the airs of love,
those ways we die.
The woman moans. Shhh,
he strums her to life,
but too much blood has spilled.
The gut contracts
and love goes
taking with it flesh.

I pocket a shard or two from scattered slabs,
pieces of a frieze washed with faint color
once spectacular, even gaudy,

the statues bleached as we are at night
strafed by the moon.

Sometimes I reach over and touch
to find if you're still flesh and whole,
no taint of history breaking in
to find us asleep, mouths open, legs spread.

Our wars are over, love, our weapons buried
where we long since agreed not to go.

Nothing to excess engraved on a wall
yet we were at our best
before exposure brought us down,
all that we were never fully retrieved,

the bronze hairs on your chest,
my hair spilled across your face.

Day ransacks the room and leaves
us breeding shadows.

...the hall fallen in decay, no talking spring,
the stream dry that had so much to say

Relics, colonnades, pedestals, strewn
between the mountain's knees.

A laurel crooks up from beneath a wall,
and splits the obdurate stone—

fragments I covet. *Drop it,*
the guard commands but I can't
leave the broken past alone, want
to enshrine it like something holy,
saving me.

by its gravity, bloody and green
in the savageness of change—

flowering camellias scorched by last night's ice,
a child carried screaming from a shelled house,
fragmented bodies identified by shreds of cloth
pulled from the line that morning and ironed.

I've said it before—whenever I hold your face
and look at you straight, I'm afraid of time so sweet.

Yet, I want you to tell me again
how true for the moment you are,
the tongue tasting my body no lie,
no powder burns on the hands gentling my fears.

Mars
a deep crimson
floating low.
An exhilaration of fireflies
      and stars
embossed on black.

Black
becoming to those of us
preparing to go out.

Late, warns the night,
time to leave.

No, not ready,
bound as I am
to the butterfly bush,
the zinnias, azaleas, and phlox,
      and you who cut
      and trim my life.

The darkened hedge, an altar
under a chalice of stars,
      particles and waves
      pouring around me—
a communion I want to share.

Will it hurt?
Will it rend
deeper than desire?

Desire kneels close
praying I won't let go.

This fruit, these glasses, these plates—
they talk to each other.

When your tongue slides over mine
I think I know everything about you—
scent, shape, desire

tilting toward us,
color rounding out flesh—
flesh with its own
shimmering nuances

   ...fruits that set the mouth watering...

and touch soft-talking us into strokes
so subtle we hardly notice
how they run into shadows,
arrangements tumbling

   ...a paring knife in the corner...

Each time we set ourselves up
is a search for perfection,
the illusion of something tangible—

a hand caressing a hip,
a moon-washed quilt
slipping to the floor,
a voice calling out.

They come to us laden,
telling of the fields they have left behind,
the rain that nourished them, the dawns.

There are changes with every light.

I could make a wardrobe
with tufts of wool
caught on thistle and bracken.

Lost—the scraps
I might have woven whole cloth.

Come watch, the man says,
shearing sheep
with the precision of long practice,
fleece, removed all of a piece,
rolled in a neat bundle.

I've been so clumsy
with people who've loved me.

Straddling a ewe,
the man props its head on his foot,
leans down with clippers,
each pass across the coat a caress.

His dogs, lying nearby,
tremble at every move—as I do,
loving the hands that have learned
to gentle the life beneath them.

Above the Dardanelles, a sprinkle of stars
and farther on, Gallipoli.
From the third floor of the hotel
I looked down on a blue canopy
lit from below,
the men gathered there singing—
a harmony I wanted to join
praising what I could only feel,
the meaning inexplicable as love's tongue.

In the silent afterglow
I thought of you at home.
In less than a month you'd be gone,
the death I refused to foresee,
weeping instead over graves of strangers,
Muslims, Christians, buried side by side.

There seemed no resolution
for our quarrels
yet we could say the word love,
each time relearning the language,
wondering how it would translate,

wondering why
I'm still locked in the spell of that night,
the city's meanness hidden in shadows,
the bay broken by reflections
that even now slap me awake.

Lie down with me,
you whispered, and I did
there in the darkness
of your dying,
our hands awkward.

The truth is
I wanted to turn away
from even that small act,
wanted you flushed and whole,
not sour flesh
no longer firm in my arms.

Silence was how we dealt
with our differences,
knowing a break can happen
before a fall,
the way old people crack
where they stand—
landing a mere
compound of fracture.

There are nights
memory invades
hollows and crevices—
a caress so insistent
my body throbs.

After your death, I wandered
country to ruined country,
in Konya waking to hear
a muezzin singing prayers,
the bent notes widening
a vacancy I can't fill.
In the market places, in alleys,
in crumbled alcoves—children.

At night they squatted
by restaurant doors,
and I'd find them there
when I left.

Buy, they begged,
and if I said no,
they insisted
Maybe tomorrow—please.
Remember me.
Remember my name.

The dead sift through us
without flesh, bone, hair,
or whatever else the stars concoct
for us to touch.

Reaching for the velvet muzzle
of a horse, their hands pass on through
never feeling the warm breath in their palms.

Try catching wind as it runs over wheat
leaving it in shocked repose.

Cruel—to see the one you love
and realize neither tongue nor limb.
Desire is an unattached shadow.

Dashing without thought against the day,
we complain at the slightest wound.
The dead drift by longing for a bruise.

Our guide is Turk-proud
though he moved from Bosnia as a child.
During the winter he's an archaeology student
on a dig at Tyre—his dig, he smiles.

This morning, newspapers proclaim
the find of another Bosnian grave,
a scramble of the unidentified.

I ask if he has a picture of his girl.
Not with him, he says, and tells us goodbye.
He'll meet her later and drive
through the night to his home in Ankara.
For him there is only one day of rest
before another tour begins.

Pull over and sleep, I advise.

In the desolate steppes ahead,
they'll lie beneath a spread of stars,
only an occasional passing car,
miles of wheat swooning on all sides—

a long whisper across the land,
the promise of grains hanging on,
feeding them for a time,
their bodies close as flesh can get,
the heart, that bloody artifact,
more difficult to find.

These are the scales we first practiced:
moist nights, leaves whispering to rain,
the pulse's quickening hum—lost

as the porcelain cup I found
on a mossy ledge in the woods,
the spring below murmuring
over watercress.

And I knelt down as we all must do
if we're to tongue the stream teasing past,
resonant with stone, silt, grass,

and excrement—often so diluted
we're unaware of the dark spill.

The true/false story of our lives,
and the voices that inhabit us, pour
from room to over-flowing room,
the aria playing itself out.

The keys on a hook by the door,
a copy made for those who are close
and careful with loss.

After tearing up the world
I'm still looking for my glasses.

Would you please remove the clip from your gun.

Let the child's limbs fly back into shape,
torn flesh mending itself.

Leave coffins stacked where they were under dust.
In the market place, let mourners bargain for spice.

The wailing you can't hear is the sorrow I've hidden,
what or who it was I wanted, lost

because I waited too long,
hunger and need shrugged off.

Listen, you say, holding my arms, *listen*.

In late afternoon clouds flatten out
so that it seems we're sailing into islands and coral seas.

Small cays, dissolving shores,
you and I island-hopping to find the coves we lost track of.

If it were possible to turn back
and start again, would we be blind as before,
still subject to the tides that set us adrift?

As a child I let myself go and floated rollers
until I was beached, sea-wash leaching a trough around my body

as if there were no undertow
to pull me beyond reprieve, as if I could escape

to play with flotsam left by the sea—wreckage
covered with oil, U-boats prowling closer than we dreamed.

Lucky for a time,
but coming up fast a towering cumulus
bulges with storms, sooner than later volatile, firing wild.

I wake to an owl screech,
black feathers scattered,
crows caterwauling around the oak,
one squawking for its lost mate.

My call came at three,
a nightmare crashing through,
your body already cool,
the tick of a fan the only hint
air once stirred with your breath.

Day took over, blazing as it did
on the wheat field where Van Gogh
shot himself, dying later
cradled in his brother's arms.

The way I held you
in a landscape I can't scumble over,

like the canvas
lashed with cobalt, ocher, black,
the one road dropped by the horizon,
the sky ominous, embittered by crows.

as if we weren't worth spying on,
night taking charge with slitted eyes,

the world drowsing off,
lurching as it slows,
you and I pulled in separate ways.

Stay, I say, coverlet and pillow
flung to the floor, the ozone torn
where we break through.

Venus in the hammock of the new moon,
Jupiter leaning over.

One more pass at love before we free-float,
reckless, taking no notice,
a throng of regrets beckoning us back.

Behind us a deep sigh,
lights turning out.

You, cycling down a dirt road,
each rut an offense,
cattle with sorrowful eyes,
a dying orchard
in the field beyond.

You, dodging the day,
afraid it might lift you
on its horns, afraid
the night might break in

and find desire
wadded in your mouth,

an impassioned letter
trampled on the floor,

the words you memorized
sliding off with the light.

A tornado rips
the skin off a town.

In the aftermath
silence

Someone facing you
wants to speak but can't quite
articulate the bad news.

A roof set down miles away.
A tattered sleeve flapping
from a stripped branch.

Everything gone
gone the woman sobs
plucking at this this
and this remnant.

The road narrows to a countryside
I've traveled before.

Around a curve the same crumbled house,
lone chimney, and jagged run of wall.

A place inhabited by weather and vista.

Say a window is open
and I'm willing to crawl through.

Once I climbed a cliff beside a waterfall,
roots and rock my ladder.
At the top I stripped and slid
into a pool.

Beyond boulders, water gave way
to a wild plunge.

And now you, my body awakened
from its long fast.
Sweet mornings, bells in the distance,
tongue, tongue, the moon, its light
dissolving into patterns
on the ceiling above our bed.

an indecent hour for those who don't mind
losing their lives in sleep.

The neighbor's dog nearly knocks me over
when I stoop to pick up the paper.

At least I'm loved
while others still dream.

Low in the sky, Venus again
fools with my heart. I stand in the dark,

half-bare, thinking of the one who died,
moonlight flooding the house.

I almost drowned until you came along
and laid me down.

The dog wants to play. Go home,
I say, the night's not done.

An unexpected opening of three orchids on a plant
that hasn't bloomed in years, a spread of white fans,
the spurred lip stained with yellow as is the cup

no bee drinks from in the room's conditioned atmosphere,
my life too in its second wind waiting for the thrust
of some random hunger, unlikely to arrive

as a trilobite to swim from stone, or for bubbles
in this crystal ball I hold to explode as they once did
when I dove, rising with them to the surface

in a silvery school of air, the sort of glitter that flashes
roadside as we drive by at 70 mph, leaving behind a whole
landscape—the aunt who each day put the house to bed,

her hand sliding across the burnished grain
of a grandfather clock, late light running down the minutes
leaving chimes for me to tend, until the hour

the pendulum suspends its swing, until the day
no horizon blocks passage into changing clouds that I,
as a child lying on sweetgrass, watch without fear.

Admit it, we're drawn to the mysterious
like this geode opened after long darkness.

A rim of agate around amethyst—
clutch of daggers, flashy lights.

What a surprise to find
the basic compounds long-solidified.

Desire, envy, spite—aren't we all here?

Geodes smoldering in a river bank.
The most coveted disclosure—

a crevice opening on murderous thoughts
vitrified, the knife stilled before the plunge,
the bomb imploding into smoky quartz.

Soil and sand are fraught with minute crystals.

Forgetful of who we are,
we walk over ourselves every day.

Remember the scene in the movie
where the strung-out vet
loses a game of Russian roulette?
After the funeral back home,
friends gather around a table, glum,
silent, waiting for coffee and beer.

Someone starts humming *God Bless America*
and they all join in, shaky and off-key.
I'm an easy weep for those endings,
can forget for a time the horror done.

Once in a motel I put my ear to the wall
and listened to the adjacent room.
Crying. A crash. Curses and moans.
Come to bed, you cajoled (soft touch, safe move),

but I wanted a fragment of that other life,
a reminder of the damaged years, the harm
still lingering on our lips, the taste for blood
that can't be kissed away.

I could barely see,
but shot at what moved,
followed blood on the leaves
to the place the buck fell,
the body still warm,
eyes not yet glazed.

Kneeling down,
I slit the throat
and pushed away
in case he kicked—
the way the dying do,
protesting to the last
regardless of pain.

Baby, my father used to say,
squeeze the trigger gentle-like.

Blood on the kitchen floor,
the smell of Neatsfoot oil,
a clean stock.

I relish the flesh
of roasted venison,
its pungent taste
bursting on the tongue.

There isn't a bone
I wouldn't gnaw
to marrow,
and suck.

Hungry, hungry—
remember that when I ease
up to you.

I want to lie in the forest
on hides stretched between poles,
my body left for birds to clean,
flesh flying off to a higher branch,

or maybe in a mound
laden with obsessions,
a brimming chalice
rather than a begging cup.

In my hand, at last, the key
to the door that kept me knocking.

Part bone, part stain,
someone's lover lies
on the earthen floor
of a burial pit, the outline
of the torso flexed
in a familiar recline
once achingly relished.

Wayward flesh
restrained by virtuous bones.

When I was young
we scavenged cemetery plots,
moved vases and flowers
to the tombstones of kin.

I wake longing for one more chance
at the turn my story might have taken
before the part I regret ran out,
my hands, even now drawing on the hours,

some lightened, some smudged
by my touch, my play,
which at any given moment
could turn on you, could bury us both.

How many times have I lent myself
to a character devised by someone else,
the voice an aside
from my own true story.

Today I ran into my reflection in a mirror,
dislocation like that of a landscape
after the painter reassigns
verities of color and line.

A second look and I was back
to my original.

Say memory is a bruise
reminding us who we harmed,
who harmed us, and why
some felt so little of the blow.

Where does it hurt—where? we ask.
The child can't always say,
leaving us frantic
to know where to lay the salve.

It's not forgiveness I want,
it's the chance to revise
the roles I failed,
the never ending chance
to play the story of myself.

When elephants come across skeletons of their dead
they stroke the length and width of bones
as if transfiguring them to a whole.

I don't know what's become of you.

Below the castle in Prague, streets twist
sternly dark, the long row of houses huddled
like frightened children, windows closed,

an occasional light in a room inhabited by someone
reading to another, a pot of tea on a table between chairs,
the history of fear subsumed by what's become of them.

Leave them where they are, you said at Melos
as I dug up bits of pottery with my nails,
the guide droning on.

In an attic I found a locket with a twine of hair.
Open and close, open, close on a conjured past
more lucid than the real and all that paled.

What's become of you I don't know.

I pocket what I can and keep it
fingered to a shine.

Yesterday is overgrown
with briars and nettles,
a graveyard, broken names.

I try to coax the past into shape
but it dissipates,
today hanging on one frangible hinge.

Show me a crimson climber
spilling over the rail
and I'll hum the day by.

I once heard a woman
singing in a field,
her voice bell-like and true
as she bent to pluck
blossoming bolls of cotton,
her hands bleeding
from wounds that had healed,
opened again, healed.

You've seen a child stop at play
to stare, as through a fog,
at some barely outlined form
not fleshed enough to recognize.

In time you'll come to understand
where your life changed and why.

Like traces of ancient earthworks—
ramparts, barrows, grids
you walk over and by, unaware—
the past becomes more penetrable
viewed from afar, relics
washed out here and there, found,
all the windswept acres resonant.

Before entering, look down
a crumbling nave to the choir,
colors from the clerestory
playing the air of all you believe,
want to believe.

Never mind the dank remainders
of the dead who fail to resurrect.

And when bells begin to chime,
never mind the small ghost
left drifting. At night it will wander

home to your arms, and when it cries
you will croon *hush hush*,
singing the runes heard
countless times, countless ways.

We play games until death comes to fetch us.
Kurt Schwitters

Who knows how far you wind
along the mountain trail
before the falls become memory,
now and then a clearing,
the sound of water—
or is it regret—cascading.

Each time you stand
drenched in spray,
a rainbow holding you tranced,
you forget the climb back
is more difficult
this year than last.

Rounding an overhang,
you're shocked
eye to eye with a buck.
Before you've had your fill,
he wheels, hooves scattering
rock, underbrush closing
over his flanks.

In the stillness,
the feral odor of Galax
rouses that deep fear,
the heaviness you sense
bearing down too fast,
your erratic heart
scrambling upslope.

You stop to rest
on the root-riddled path
that has drawn you up
as often as let you down.
The sun leaves ash, the moon
splits between clouds,
stars ticking on and off.
You hardly notice
how weather picks you to shreds.

Hours, days, years
pass in this wilderness.
You begin to sing out
the bell-tones of sorrel,
bluets, lobelia, trillium.
The way it is at night
when a child kneels for prayers,
calling all the names he loves
before the lights switch off.

Dreams stay busy all night
changing into this costume or that.
Hold me, a lover dares, but the fickle scenes
dump us from bed to unmade bed.

Good morning, I'm able to say—
the day's felt hammer
striking a taut wire.

Dancing around the sphere
of a bar-room floor,
I press as close to you as I can,
your breath in my hair.

Time for bed, you whisper
and I shiver for the one who'll wake
to find the other not there,

the unfinished script improvising
another day into night,
stars again making an entrance.

The moment of suspense—
a threshold we linger on
before we're whirled out
beyond control, beyond care.

The letter A is a tent that held us for a while.
Now we're restless to leave the alphabet
and ride off into numbers.

But numbers can't divine
the luminous grove we could happen upon,
you and I stretched on the same sliver of time,
its stream winding down into fragrance,
our shadows now plaited, now loose.

In the warm intersection of sex and love,
the mouth puckers as soon as we're born,
starved no matter how often and deep
we push into someone else.

Numbers tell how we come and go
yet fail to fathom a woman's grief
as she tosses on a bed she can't fill.

The purity of numbers deceives us
into thinking they're true,
could never be found in a stranger's arms.

Numbers wasted on wars
rough up the contours of history,
the landscape defined by a blast of white,
the grass we greened gone, the mare
no longer nuzzling the child's palm.

Maybe Voyager, floating in its frigid sea of stars,
will land and voices once more disembark.
Absurd to think our slow-motion scatter of dust
is the beginning and end of words
announcing we've come, we've gone.

A loop of universe caught
by the swing of a telescope,
galaxies swirling out like words
when a rose becomes more
than scent or thorn,

the finger bleeding,
the mouth sucking its own
sweet fluidity, your tongue
covering mine, the body
shivering to recover its focus.

Beyond that I can't think,

can only hold on
to Joseph Cornell's
Starfish construction
which shifts with each shake
of the frame, the beach scene
never again repeating,

just as our footprints
disappear with the tide
that first brought us in.

So many unwitting escapes—
the universe handled blindly
until conjured
from a wheel of equations.

In Vermeer's painting
of *Woman Holding a Balance*,
a flick of white on the scales
streaks through the darkness.

The pearls strewn across the table—
sublime little worlds
we imagine picked up by chance,

someone warm like you or me
holding them to the light
before trying them on,

their lustre increased
when they rest against flesh,
the throat pulsing,
the voice flying out.

From the edge of the woods to the oak,
the pear tree, and now the roof,
the owl is all over us tonight,
and farther the stars
tossing us out in the cold.

From our warren of a bed, it's easy to forget
the agnostic bones hidden in believable flesh
our fingers insist on exploring,

the ranting of hands a Braille, touch
trying to spell more than is there
each time we approach the verbs of love.

When we climbed the hill to Cueva de la Pileta,
a sputtering lamp led to animals, grids,
hands, outlined on stone, the passage mute
except for our chatter.

To save ourselves from erasure,
we change the subject to an answerable code,
a word or gesture that allows us
into the body of all we live,

labyrinths sometimes losing us,
sometimes leading us into a sanctum,
the ones we've loved rising from their sleep,
not whole, but an aura
we wrap ourselves in when weathers turn.

Twice as a child I was shaken out of myself.
A squall of light blew over and through me,
the surrounding world shimmering alive,
all things equal—leaf, house, bird—
and I was touched as no one, nothing,
has touched me since, casting ever after
for repeat of that call.

The Song of the Horse ▲	Samuel Hazo
My Life as a Doll	Elizabeth Kirschner
She Heads into the Wilderness	Anne Marie Macari
When She Named Fire:	
An Anthology of Contemporary	
Poetry by American Women	Andrea Hollander Budy, ed.
67 Mogul Miniatures	Raza Ali Hasan
House Where a Woman	Lori Wilson
A Theory of Everything	Mary Crockett Hill
• 2008, selected by Naomi Shihab Nye	
What the Heart Can Bear	Robert Gibb
The Working Poet: 75 Writing	
Exercises and a Poetry	
Anthology	Scott Minar, ed.
Blood Honey	Chana Bloch
The White Museum	George Bilgere
The Gift That Arrives Broken	Jacqueline Berger
• 2009, selected by Alicia Ostriker	
Farang	Peter Blair
Shake It and It Snows ★	Gailmarie Pahmeier
The Ghetto Exorcist ★	James Tyner
Where the Road Turns	Patricia Jabbeh Wesley
To Make It Right	Corrinne Clegg Hales
• 2010, selected by Claudia Emerson	
The Autumn House Anthology of	
Contemporary American Poetry,	
Second Edition	Michael Simms, ed.
Coda	Marilyn Donnelly
Crossing Laurel Run ★	Maxwell King
Shelter ★	Gigi Marks
The Torah Garden	Philip Terman
Lie Down with Me: New and	
Selected Poems	Julie Suk

• Winner of the annual Autumn House Poetry Prize
▲ Hardcover
★ *Coal Hill Review* Chapbook

Cover and text design by Kathy Boykowycz

Set in Minion fonts, designed in 1990 by Robert Slimbach

Printed by McNaughton & Gunn on Nature's Book,
a 30% recycled paper